Biography®

Mohandas GANDHI

Christopher Martin

Lerner Publications Company
Minneapolis

Lerner Publications Company
A division of Lerner Publishing Group
241 First Avenue North
Minneapolis, MN 55401 U.S.A.

Website address: www.lernerbooks.com

Library of Congress Cataloging-in-Publication Data

Martin, Christopher, 1923–
    Mohandas Gandhi / by Christopher Martin.
        p.   c.m — (A&E biography)
    Includes bibliographical references and index.
    Summary: Details the life of India's most noted spiritual leader, Mohandas Gandhi.
    ISBN 0-8225-4984-0 (lib. bdg. : alk. paper)
    1. Gandhi, Mahatma, 1869–1948. 2. Statesmen—India Biography.
3. Nationalists—India Biography. I. Title. II. Series.
DS481.G3M317   2001
954.03'5'092—dc21
    [B]   99-28431

Manufactured in the United States of America
1 2 3 4 5 6 – JR – 06 05 04 03 02 01

CONTENTS

Mohandas Gandhi was driven by a belief that all people should be free to live in a world without violence or hatred.

INTRODUCTION

The train carrying Mohandas Gandhi, an Indian lawyer practicing in South Africa in 1893, reached the city of Pietermaritzburg at about 9 p.m. A fellow passenger stared at Gandhi, noting that he was a "colored man," although he was dressed in a European-style suit. The passenger left the train car and came back with two railroad officials. In South Africa at the time, blacks, Indians, and Asians were not allowed to travel, live, attend school, or otherwise mix with white South Africans.

A third official came into the train car and told Gandhi to go to the third-class compartment. Gandhi told him he had a first-class ticket and refused to leave. The official told Gandhi he would call a police officer to push him out of the compartment if he did not leave it. Gandhi told him to go ahead and call the police office because he would not leave voluntarily.

A police officer arrived. He took Gandhi by the hand and pushed him out of the compartment. His luggage was confiscated by railroad authorities. The train steamed away. Gandhi sat in the waiting room of the railway station with only a small suitcase.

It was winter in South Africa. Pietermaritzburg, located in the mountains, was bitterly cold. Gandhi's overcoat was stored in his luggage. He dared not ask for it, fearing he would be insulted again.

Gandhi during his years as a lawyer in South Africa

Should he fight for his rights, or should he ignore the insults? Should he go back to India and forget the injustices in South Africa? Gandhi decided that it would be cowardly to return to India. He decided to stay in South Africa—and he stayed for three years, fighting a battle for racial tolerance. In the process, he determined his life's course as an apostle of freedom.

Gandhi at age seven. He was a shy child and often ran home as soon as school was over for fear of running into bullies.

Chapter **ONE**

A Boy in British India

AT THE TIME OF **MOHANDAS GANDHI'S BIRTH IN** 1869, India was ruled by Great Britain. India was a huge country and home to 300 million people speaking twelve main languages. Its population was divided among seven major religions: Hinduism, Islam, Sikhism, Jainism, Buddhism, Mazdaism, and Christianity. People of these different religions, as well as of different races, lived together in reasonable harmony—but to say that they all were happy would be far from the truth.

India had been ruled by Hindus until the thirteenth century, when Muslim rulers displaced them. Muslims held power until the middle of the sixteenth century, when Portugal took control of the state of Bombay and parts of India's west coast. England gained a foothold in India through marriage. In 1662 the seven islands that comprise the state of Bombay were given to the English king Charles II as a wedding gift for his marriage to a Portuguese princess. Six years later, for a small yearly payment, the East India Company acquired the islands from the English Crown (king).

The East India Company was a private English firm authorized by the government to do business in Asia. The company soon became very rich and powerful. "We did not conquer India for the benefit of the Indians," a British politician observed centuries later. "We conquered India as an outlet for the goods of Great Britain."

From this beginning, British power, influence, and territory steadily increased in India. In 1858 Britain took control of India from the East India Company, and India became a British colony. It was governed by a British viceroy, appointed by the Crown, and native (Indian) princes. The British government, called the Raj, maintained peace and provided a degree of unity, law, and stability to India. But the people of India wanted independence. To achieve it, they needed a leader.

THE DEWAN'S SON

Such a leader was born into a Hindu family on October 2, 1869, in a small seaside town in India called Porbandar, about halfway between the cities of Bombay and Karachi. The child's name was Mohandas Karamchand Gandhi.

As the chief minister of the city-state of Porbandar, India, Gandhi's father, left, was known for his honesty.

Mohandas's father, Karamchand Gandhi, was the dewan, or chief minister, of the Porbandar city-state. (It consisted of the town of Porbandar and the surrounding region.) In this position, Karamchand assisted the ruling princes of Porbandar. He had no formal education or training in politics, but he was incorruptible and brought honor to the family. Mohandas might have been expected to follow his father into the service of local princes. Instead, he devoted his life to the service of the common people.

Gandhi had two older brothers and an older sister. He recalled that his mother, Putlibai, was a devout

Hindu who attended services every day and never ate a meal without praying. She fasted often, and during Chaturmas, a Hindu holiday that lasted through India's four-month rainy season, she ate only one meal a day. Gandhi learned from his mother that fasting represented self-discipline and self-purification.

Hinduism divided people into four main castes, or classes, based on social position. The Brahmans, or priests, made up the highest caste. The second

Gandhi's mother, Putlibai

ranking caste was the Kshatriyas, rulers and warriors, and the third was the Vaishyas, merchants and farmers. The fourth caste, the Sudras, were laborers. The Gandhis were members of the Vaishyas—the merchant caste. The family had originally been grocers. The name Gandhi means "grocer" in Hindi, one of the many languages of northern India.

Below the four castes were the outcastes, or untouchables. They were the poorest of India's poor. They worked cleaning toilets and stables. They could not draw water from the town's common well. They could only use filthy water from the sewers. Untouchables could not enter Hindu temples. They lived in the lowest quarters of the worst slums. If a devout Hindu even touched an untouchable or anything the untouchable had touched, he or she had to undergo ritual purification, which involved prayer and cleansing the body.

Everything in Hindu life was ruled by the caste system, and a caste was permanent. If you were born a Brahman, you remained a Brahman. If you were born an untouchable, you died an untouchable. According to Hindu belief, caste was the reward or punishment for conduct in a previous existence. Only in heaven could your status be changed for your soul's next life on earth.

In addition to the main castes, Hindu society was controlled by subcastes. The head of each subcaste, guided by a ruling council, controlled the lives of its

Gandhi's birthplace in Porbandar, India. Not only did Gandhi's parents and siblings live in the house, but his uncles and their families also lived there.

members. Gandhi's family belonged to the Modha Bania subcaste, a group that would later cause him considerable trouble.

The extended family was the foundation of Hindu society, however. Mohandas lived in a big house with his parents, his siblings, his father's brothers, and their families. There was little strife in the household. Karamchand was the patriarch, and his rule was law.

The Gandhis were more prosperous than most Indians. They had household servants and homes in the city-states of Porbandar, Rajkot, and Kutiana. At one time or another, Karamchand was the dewan of each of these city-states.

EARLY LESSONS

Mohandas was a small child with big ears and deep-set eyes. Starting at age five, he went to school in Porbandar. By his own admission, he was a slow learner, and he had particular trouble with multiplication tables.

In 1876 the family moved to Rajkot, about one hundred miles inland from Porbandar. Karamchand became the dewan of that city-state, but it was not as pleasant as Porbandar. In Rajkot, the Gandhi family lived in a three-story stone house with a small courtyard, in a compound surrounded by a high wall. Karamchand, Putlibai, and their four children lived in just two rooms on the ground floor. The extended family of aunts, uncles, and cousins lived in the rest of the house.

It was here that Gandhi first became aware of segregation. He saw that the British reserved the best sections of Rajkot for themselves. The British neighborhoods had paved roads, gardens, sewers, running water, and parks. The Indian section of the city was fly-ridden, filthy, and stank of urine and garbage. Families drew their water from wells. Even though Karamchand was dewan of the city-state, the Gandhis' neighborhood was a slum. The Indian people were deliberately humiliated in their own country.

Mohandas was sent to the local elementary school, where he studied arithmetic, geography, Gujarati (his native language), Sanskrit (the ancient language of the Hindu religion), and Persian (an ancient language of the Islamic religion practiced by Muslims). Because India was a British colony, Mohandas also studied English. He was a shy child who ran home as soon as lessons were over, afraid that he would be bullied. "My books and my lessons were my sole companions," he recalled later.

Life in Rajkot was simple. The family rose with the dawn and made their ablutions, or ritual baths. They dressed in traditional cotton clothing, with only shawls to protect them from cold weather. They followed strict Hindu dietary laws that forbade the eating of meat—an observant Hindu would not kill any living creature, not even an insect. Everyone in the family went to bed early, except for Karamchand. He sometimes sat up half the night talking about politics or religion with his friends.

As Mohandas grew older, he made friends and enjoyed games—spinning tops, throwing balloons, and playing a kind of field hockey in the streets. He also developed some bad habits. He began smoking when he was twelve and even stole money from his parents and siblings to buy cigarettes. One of his brothers had a golden bracelet, and Mohandas clipped little pieces from it to sell for tobacco. Finally, he recognized his wrongdoing and wrote a confession to his father.

He trembled as he handed the confession to his father, who was ill at the time, but he sat up in bed to read it. As Karamchand read the note, he wept and tore up the paper. There would be no punishment. Mohandas also wept, for he could see his father's unhappiness. This event was Gandhi's introduction to ahimsa, the Hindu principle of nonviolence. For Gandhi, ahimsa would become a basic law of life.

Gandhi, left, and a schoolmate pose for this photo taken in Rajkot, India, in about 1883.

Chapter **TWO**

THE YOUNG HUSBAND

CAREFREE BOYHOOD ENDED FOR **MOHANDAS GANDHI** in 1882, when he was thirteen years old. That is the year he married—childhood marriage was common in Hindu society. His bride was Kasturbai Nakanji, also thirteen. Although the couple did not know it, they had been engaged for six years. The marriage had been arranged by their families.

Kasturbai was a strong girl with a powerful personality. She was shy, simple, and persevering. Like many Indian girls, she had never learned to read. Mohandas eventually taught her enough Gujarati that she could read and write simple letters.

Because of the role of the extended family in Indian society, Mohandas and Kasturbai did not have to set up their own household. They lived with Gandhi's parents, as well as his uncles and their wives and children. At least Mohandas and his wife had their own room.

"I lost no time in assuming the authority of a husband," Gandhi said. "Immediately I told Kasturbai she could not go outside the compound without my permission." But Kasturbai rejected his order, and there was a quarrel—the first of many in their stormy marriage. Gandhi was a jealous husband, and Kasturbai was an independent wife. Sometimes they did not speak to one another for several days at a time.

What's more, Kasturbai was physically bigger and stronger than her husband. He was short, thin, and weak. She was fearless, while he was afraid of the dark, snakes, and even goblins that he thought were lurking in the dark.

Because he was so small, Gandhi disliked sports such as cricket and gymnastics, which were required activities in his school. Knowing that he must have some exercise, he took long walks, which made him stronger. But he envied athletic boys. One boy he particularly envied was Sheik Mehtab, a Muslim friend who was big and strong and excelled in track and field. Mehtab did not quake·at the thought of ghosts and snakes. What was the secret of his strength, Gandhi wondered. It was, he decided, that Mehtab ate meat.

Hindus were forbidden to eat meat, and Gandhi had never tasted it. Some people even blamed this dietary restriction for India's subordination to a foreign power. "Behold the mighty Englishman," exclaimed one English poem, "He rules the Indian small/Because being a meat eater/He is five cubits tall."

A rebellious young man, Mohandas decided that he would try eating meat. But he had strong reservations about breaking religious laws. And he did not want his family to discover his misdeed. It would have to be a very secret experiment, conducted in out-of-the-way places that his family did not go to. One day, he and Sheik Mehtab went to a river for a picnic. Mehtab produced some cooked goat, which Gandhi ate. After he swallowed it, he threw up. That night he dreamed of a bleating goat in his belly. Still, he kept eating meat with Sheik Mehtab. Finally, he became ashamed of his dishonesty and quit, never to eat meat again.

By eating meat, Gandhi had rebelled not only against his family but also against his religion. He believed in God, but he disliked Hindu temples with their many icons (religious objects) and rituals. He did not believe what he read in the sacred Hindu books. He listened to his father's discussions with members of various religions, but he was not convinced that any one group had the key to salvation.

Mohandas was impressed by Jain beliefs, though. Jainism, an offshoot of Hinduism, taught nonviolence toward all living things. Jain priests wore gauze masks to avoid accidentally inhaling and killing an insect.

They did not go out at night to avoid unwittingly stepping on a worm.

RITES OF PASSAGE

Karamchand Gandhi died in 1885. Mohandas then enrolled in Samaldas College in the city of Bhavnagar, not far from Rajkot. But lectures there were given in English, and Mohandas had trouble understanding them. At the end of the first term, he returned home, uncertain about his career. He was interested in medicine, but his religion objected to the dissection of cadavers. His brother Laxmidas suggested law and politics. Both their father and grandfather had been dewans to the princes of Porbandar. If Mohandas became a lawyer, he would likely follow in their footsteps.

An old family friend, a Brahman, advised Mohandas to go to England for a three-year law course. He could study to become a barrister, a lawyer in the superior courts. Gandhi's mother did not want him to go abroad for three years. But the excitement of foreign travel appealed to the young man.

Another person was against the plan. Mohandas's uncle Tulsidas said that European-trained Indian lawyers "dressed as shamelessly as Englishmen, abandoned the Hindu traditions and were never seen without a cigar in their mouths." Karamchand had recently died, so Uncle Tulsidas was now head of the family. His word was law.

Still, if Gandhi's mother agreed, Uncle Tulsidas

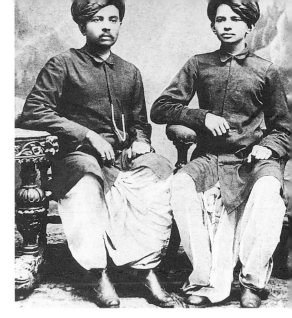

Gandhi, right, *with his elder brother, Laxmidas, at Samaldas College in Bhavnagar, India, in 1886*

would approve of the experiment. Putlibai also had doubts about the morality of young men in England. A Jain monk administered an oath by which Mohandas promised that he would not touch wine, women, or meat while he was studying abroad.

Laxmidas, already working as a solicitor (a lawyer in the lower courts), provided the money for Mohandas's schooling. He accompanied Mohandas to Bombay, where he was to board a ship for England. But when the brothers reached the city, they met with opposition from other members of the extended family—elders of the Modha Bania subcaste. No Modha Bania had ever been to England before. Hinduism could not be practiced there, said the elders. Mohandas could not go. They called a family meeting in Bombay, and Mohandas was called to appear before them.

The sheth (elder) told Gandhi his request was not proper. He said their religion forbade travel abroad. He had heard that it was impossible to live in

England without compromising the Hindu faith, as people felt obliged to eat and drink with Europeans.

Mohandas rebelled. He was going to England, he said. He had made a solemn vow to his mother to keep the faith. The sheth told Gandhi it was impossible to keep their religion in England and to listen to his advice.

Gandhi told the sheth he could not alter his resolve to go to England. He pointed out that his mother and brother, along with a learned Brahman, had given him permission to go.

When the sheth asked Gandhi if he was going to disregard the orders of the caste, Gandhi told him he thought the caste should not interfere in this matter.

This reply angered the sheth. He swore at Gandhi, but the young man remained unmoved. The sheth then disowned Mohandas. He ordered that any one who helped Gandhi or saw him off at the dock would · be punished with a fine.

This cruel statement seared the soul of young Gandhi, and he never forgot it. His own family had called him an outcaste. This declaration gave him a hatred of the caste system and a sympathy for the real outcastes, the untouchables.

He persisted in his rebellion. He bought a ticket to London, a British jacket, two British suits, a necktie, and enough food for the three-week sea voyage to Southampton. He sailed from Bombay on September 4, 1888, one month before his nineteenth birthday. He was already a father. Several months earlier, Kasturbai had delivered a son named Harilal. While Mohandas studied in England, his wife and son would stay in Rajkot with the rest of the family. Meanwhile, the young father was setting out on a long journey— longer than he knew.

In an effort to fit in, Gandhi dressed and acted the part of a perfect English gentleman while studying law in London. Despite his attempts to belong, he still felt like an outcast in the city.

Chapter **THREE**

BARRISTER GANDHI

ON THE VOYAGE TO SOUTHAMPTON, GANDHI KEPT mostly to himself. He spoke very little English, and he was shy about talking, even to the ship's steward. He spent much of his time hanging on the ship's rail, watching the movement of the sea. At mealtime, he usually ate in his cabin because he didn't know how to use a knife and fork. In India he had eaten with his fingers, as was the common cultural practice. He ate mostly his own food because he didn't know whether or not dishes prepared in the ship's kitchen contained meat. If the steward brought him a piece of meat, Gandhi sent it back.

The ship arrived at Southampton on a Saturday. Gandhi was presented with a bill for all the uneaten meals, which he paid. He had set aside a white flannel suit friends had given to him for the trip to London. But he did not know about the English habit of switching from white to colored clothing on the first of September. When he arrived at the Victoria Hotel, he was dreadfully embarrassed to see that he was the only person in the lobby wearing white.

Gandhi had arrived in London armed with letters of introduction—notes from Indian contacts introducing him to colleagues in England. But being shy, he seldom made use of the letters. He did send one, a note to Dr. P. J. Mehta, a medical doctor from Bombay. Dr. Mehta called on Gandhi at the Victoria Hotel, smiling to see the young man dressed in white flannel. Dr. Mehta then gave Gandhi some useful advice on English etiquette: Don't touch the belongings of others. Don't ask questions of new acquaintances. Don't talk in a loud voice. Don't address other men as "Sir," a title used only by servants and subordinates in addressing their masters.

THE ENGLISH GENTLEMAN

The London to which Gandhi had come was a splendid city at the height of its glory. At the fancy Pall Mall Club, gentlemen sipped sherry and reminded one another that "the sun never sets on the British Empire." Queen Victoria sat on the throne. And of all the British colonies—the jewels in Victoria's crown—the brightest was "the Star of India."

England's Queen Victoria in 1887

Gandhi was enrolled at the Inner Temple, a London law school. In the course of his studies, his English improved, as did his knowledge of the law, politics, and Indian history. But Gandhi was intent on learning to become an English gentleman as well as a barrister. He began to read London newspapers, although he had rarely read newspapers in India. He bought a top hat, a morning coat, striped trousers, and a walking stick decorated with silver. Soon he had all the accessories of an English gentleman—silk shirts, leather gloves, and evening clothes tailored on fashionable Bond Street. But the transformation did not work.

When Gandhi had his photograph taken a few weeks after his arrival, the picture showed a young Indian masquerading as a European—a young man with thick black hair parted to the right and clothing that was obviously uncomfortable.

In search of belonging, he paid for dancing lessons, but he found he could not put rhythm into his feet. He bought a violin and studied with a teacher. But the music lessons were no more successful than the dancing lessons, and the violin was soon sold. He began a course in elocution, or public speaking, which was also soon abandoned. His efforts to become an English gentleman were a failure. He did not have the background to fit seamlessly into his surroundings. He remained an outsider, a young Indian pretending to be an Englishman.

SPIRITUAL AWAKENINGS

Eventually, though, Gandhi found his place in London. Determined not to eat meat, he sought out vegetarian restaurants and joined London's Vegetarian Society. Its members experimented with a number of dietary fads. Gandhi began to study their ideas and to renounce certain foods, partly to save money, partly for self-discipline. He cut out spices and sweets and began to enjoy simple foods such as boiled spinach prepared without seasoning. "Many such experiments taught me that the real seat of taste was not the tongue but the mind," he said.

He also began a study of world religions, starting with Hinduism, the religion of his birth. He read the Bhagavad Gita, a Hindu holy book, and came across several ideas that fascinated him. One was the concept of nonpossession—the giving up of material goods and personal desires in order to awaken the spirit.

A Christian friend suggested that he read the Bible, so he did, starting with the Book of Genesis. He found that the Old Testament didn't hold his attention. But the New Testament kept his attention, particularly the

Gandhi, a lifelong vegetarian, joined London's Vegetarian Society while studying law in England. He is seated in the first row on the right.

Sermon on the Mount. In this sermon, Jesus advises his followers to "turn the other cheek" when assaulted and "to love your enemies." This message would guide Gandhi's actions in the years to come.

STORMY TRANSITION

Upon graduation from law school, Gandhi was admitted to the English bar—the official association of barristers. He enrolled in the bar on June 11, 1891. The next day he sailed for India aboard the SS *Assam*.

He came home eager to see his mother. But his brother Laxmidas met him at the dock with the sad news that she had died while Gandhi was in London. The family had not told him because they knew how upset he would be. The shock was great, but Gandhi put his grief aside, determined to show his brother that he could succeed. He was reunited with Kasturbai, although the three-year separation had not done much to improve their marriage. Gandhi was possessive of his wife and often jealous. The couple argued frequently.

The controversy within the family's subcaste had not subsided. Gandhi was still condemned by the family in Bombay, but this time he made no move to resist them. He was now practicing ahimsa, the theory of nonviolence. If he was insulted, he would not return the insults. If he was criticized, he would not reply in kind. To meet force with force and violence with violence would only cause relationships to deteriorate further, Gandhi believed.

Gandhi was advised to set up a law practice in Bombay. Laxmidas, a solicitor, did his best to send business to his brother. But Gandhi would not open his office until he felt competent to practice law. He had no confidence in his skills at the beginning.

Finally, he got a case. It was to be tried in Small Causes Court, with Barrister Gandhi representing the defendant. He would have to cross-examine the witnesses for the plantiff (opposition), but he was too frightened to do so. He told the judge to find another barrister for the defense. Ashamed of himself for failing, he vowed not to take a case again until he had gathered enough courage to appear in court.

He looked for another job to support himself in the meantime. After three years in London, he spoke English fluently. He applied for a job as an English teacher but was rejected because he did not have the necessary degree. In despair, he closed his house and office in Bombay and moved back to Rajkot, setting up a new practice. There, he was more successful. Most of his work involved drafting legal documents on behalf of the poor. His success came in part because his brother Laxmidas sent him clients.

It was during this time that Gandhi had his first encounter with the British Raj. Laxmidas, secretary and adviser to the prince of Porbandar, had angered the prince. The matter had gone to the local British agent (government official), a man who disliked Laxmidas. Gandhi had known the agent in London on a friendly basis. He went to plead his brother's case, but the agent would not listen. Gandhi persisted, and the Englishman threw Barrister Gandhi out of his office.

This time, Gandhi did not practice ahimsa. He wrote a letter complaining of mistreatment and threatening legal action. He received an angry reply. Not knowing how to proceed, Gandhi sought the advice of Pherozeshah Mehta, an Indian politician in Bombay.

HINDUISM

Hinduism, the main religion of India, is a complex belief system involving many gods and goddesses. Its roots are in Vedism, the religion of ancient India.

The three most important Hindu gods are Brahma (creator of the universe), Vishnu (protector of humanity), and Shiva (a god who periodically destroys the world and then recreates it). Their stories are told in a number of sacred texts, including the Bhagavad Gita (the book that guided Ghandi's spiritual path) and the four Vedas, or Books of Knowledge.

A number of beliefs guide Hindu life. One is the concept of reincarnation—the idea that the soul never dies but instead is reborn after death into a new body. The process is said to be repeated again and again until the soul achieves spiritual perfection. Hindus hope to achieve this state through good works. Hinduism also teaches ahimsa, or nonviolence, and the giving up of material goods. All of these teachings influenced Gandhi and guided his social, spiritual, and political quests.

Mehta advised Gandhi to drop the matter. An Indian could never get the better of a British colonial official, he was told. To proceed with his grievance was to court disaster. Forget the insult, Mehta said. This advice disturbed Gandhi, but he followed it.

Gandhi did not like that Indian society was filled with political intrigues and complexities that he could not understand. His brother offered him a way out: One of Laxmidas's clients needed a barrister in South Africa. Was Gandhi interested in the job? He would be given a round-trip boat ticket, payment for expenses, and one-year's salary. Gandhi jumped at the offer.

In his early twenties, Gandhi, third from left, *worked as a lawyer in South Africa.*

Chapter **FOUR**

STRUGGLE IN SOUTH AFRICA

IN APRIL 1893, MOHANDAS GANDHI ARRIVED IN Durban, in the province of Natal in South Africa. Once again, Kasturbai remained in India. Gandhi's new employer, Dada Abdulla Sheth, met him at the dock. Gandhi had been hired to represent Dada Abdulla and Company in court. But as an Indian in South Africa, Gandhi was soon to face battles far greater than anything he would encounter in a court of law.

Like India, South Africa at the time was under British rule. A group of Dutch settlers called Boers were fighting for self-rule in the region. Racial segregation in the colony was extreme. Native blacks had no rights and were subordinate to their white European rulers.

Indians, Asians, and people of mixed blood were called "coloreds." Their social status was only slightly higher than that of black South Africans.

Thousands of Indians lived in South Africa, many were laborers who had immigrated to work on British farms. The rights of the Indians varied from province to province. In some places, Indians could be employed only as waiters and porters. Laws prevented them from voting, owning land in most areas, or even walking on city streets after dark. The Transvaal re-

Gandhi, second row third from right, **with members of the Indian Ambulance Corps, which he organized to help the British during the Boer War in South Africa.**

gion had particularly oppressive laws. The British called all Indians "coolies," from the Hindi word *kuli,* which means "laborer." Thus Gandhi became known as "the coolie barrister."

His confrontation with European authority began almost immediately. Two days after arriving in South Africa, Gandhi went to a Durban court wearing a turban, a traditional Indian headdress. The magistrate asked him to remove the turban. According to South African law, Indians had to remove their hats in the presence of white Europeans. Gandhi refused and left the courtroom. Thereafter, he wore his turban constantly and did not remove it until ordered to do so by the chief justice of Natal's supreme court. Other Indians did not like Gandhi's submission to the court. They felt it was a sign of weakness. But Gandhi wanted to reserve his strength for bigger battles.

The next confrontation came in Pietermaritzburg. On the way to Johannesburg, Gandhi was ejected from a train for refusing to move from the first- to the third-class compartment. After sitting up all night in the Pietermaritzburg train station, Gandhi wired his boss, who complained to railway authorities in Durban.

Although Gandhi was given first-class treatment on the next train, to Charlestown, he was mistreated again upon transfer to a stagecoach. The coach operator would not allow him to enter. He was forced to ride on top with the driver and was later ordered to sit on the coach's footboard to make room for a European passenger. When he refused, the coach operator began to beat and threaten him. Gandhi did not resist this treatment but instead practiced ahimsa—nonviolence.

Arriving in Johannesburg, Gandhi went to a hotel. He was told the hotel was full. An Indian client later asked him how he ever expected to be admitted to a hotel. Gandhi asked him why. "You will come to know after you have stayed here a few days," the man answered. "Only we can live in a land like this, because, for making money, we [Indians] do not mind pocketing insults and here we are."

Indeed, the insults continued. In Pretoria, a policeman kicked Gandhi off a public street. Indians were not allowed out after 9:00 P.M. without a permit. An American friend witnessed the incident and offered to support Gandhi's protest in court. But Gandhi refused the offer. He would practice ahimsa. His religious spirit was awakened.

CHANGE OF PLANS

In Natal, Gandhi continued his study of religions, including Christianity. He also learned much about the lawyer's trade, particularly that legal costs can eat up all the advantages of winning a case. Therefore, he realized, compromise was often better than victory.

By the spring of 1894, Gandhi's contract with Dada Abdulla and Company was coming to a close. His second son, Manilal, had been born in India on October 28, 1892. Gandhi wanted to go home.

In Durban to prepare for his return trip, Gandhi learned of a bill that would deprive Natal's Indians of their franchise—the right to vote in provincial elections. "If this bill passes into law it will make our lot extremely difficult," Gandhi told Dada Abdulla Sheth at his farewell party. "It is the first nail into our coffin. It strikes at the root of our self-respect."

Other guests at the party heard Gandhi's remarks. One of them told Gandhi he should cancel his trip home and stay a month longer to direct them how to fight.

Others chimed in, begging Gandhi to lead the fight for Indian rights. As the pleas mounted, Gandhi was convinced to stay put. "Thus God laid the foundations of my life in South Africa and sowed the seed of the fight for national self-respect," he wrote. Soon, about twenty Indian merchants hired Gandhi for legal work, and Dada Abdulla bought him the furniture necessary for a law office. Gandhi remained in Natal.

THE FIGHT BEGINS

The franchise bill had already passed its first reading in the legislature. The fact that no Indians had expressed opposition during the reading was said to be proof of their unfitness to vote. In an effort to delay passage of the legislation, Gandhi sent telegrams to the speaker of the assembly, the prime minister, and several prominent legislators. In just two weeks, he led an effort to get ten thousand signatures on a petition for Indian voting rights in Natal. The franchise bill passed, and the cause put new life into South Africa's Indian community.

Consulting with friends, Gandhi moved to establish a permanent political organization, the Natal Indian Congress. The group would attempt to educate the English in South Africa, England, and India about the plight of Indians in Natal. As secretary of the congress, Gandhi wrote two pamphlets, both widely circulated. One was a general description of the treatment of Indians in Natal. The other, *The Indian Franchise—An Appeal,* concerned Indian voting rights. South Africa's Indians were ready for action.

By mid-1896, Gandhi had been separated from his wife and children for almost three years. He appointed an assistant to handle his duties as secretary of the Natal Indian Congress and sailed for Calcutta. Back in India, Gandhi continued his work, writing about the conditions he had witnessed in South Africa. In late 1886, he returned to South Africa, this time accompanied by his wife, his two sons, and the ten-year-old son of his widowed sister.

When Gandhi's ship landed in Natal, it was put under quarantine—held in the harbor for fear that passengers were carrying disease. In fact, authorities were trying to have Gandhi banned from South Africa altogether. The tactic did not work. After more than three weeks in quarantine, the passengers were allowed to leave the ship.

Gandhi's wife, Kasturbai, center, *is pictured here with their four sons.* From left to right: *Harilal, Ramdas, Kasturbai, Devadas, and Manilal*

But word of Gandhi's activities had spread among white South Africans. After sending Kasturbai and the children ahead separately, Gandhi was met by a group of whites bent on violence. "We'll hang old Gandhi/On a sour apple tree," the crowd sang. Disguised as an Indian policeman and accompanied by two detectives, Gandhi managed to escape to a police station for safety.

The crowd soon became a mob, which organized a search of the house where Gandhi's family was staying. When they did not find him, they dispersed. Authorities wanted to prosecute the leaders of the mob, but Gandhi refused to press charges.

The family settled in Durban, where Kasturbai gave birth to another son, Ramdas, in 1897. Gandhi volunteered his services at a hospital for the poor. For two hours every morning, he attended to Indian patients and helped explain their symptoms to the doctors.

In 1899 the Boers who had been fighting to control South Africa rebelled against British authority in a series of raids. Britain sent a force to quell the uprising, and war was declared on October 11. Although Gandhi sympathized with the Boers' desire for self-rule, his loyalty to Great Britain drove him to support the British cause. He organized an Indian ambulance corps—1,100 strong. In battle, the corps marched as many as 25 miles per day, carrying the wounded on stretchers to medical tents. For this work, corps leaders were awarded the British War Medal.

When his next child was about to be born the following year, neither a doctor nor a midwife was available, and Gandhi had to deliver the baby himself. It was a son, whom they named Devadas. Gandhi's relationship with Kasturbai remained rocky.

To India and Back

When the war ended with the Boers' surrender, Gandhi concluded that his work was no longer in South Africa but in India. He sailed home and spent several weeks traveling around the country, seeking support for the Indians in South Africa. In 1901, the Indian National Congress, a party organized to fight for Indian independence, held a convention in Calcutta. There, Gandhi presented a resolution calling for the assistance of South African Indians. The resolution passed unanimously. Gandhi had won the backing of the most important Indian leaders.

Though he was devoted to the fight for justice in South Africa, Gandhi could no longer ignore the problems in his own country. One was poor sanitation. On the first day of the Congress meeting in Calcutta, Gandhi went to the toilets and was dismayed to find them filthy, stinking, and full of waste. Some delegates didn't use the toilets at all but simply soiled the porches outside their rooms. Gandhi spoke to convention organizers about cleaning the toilets. "That is not our work," they replied. "It is the work of the scavengers [untouchables]." Gandhi demanded a broom and proceeded to clean the toilets himself. He knew that if sanitation in India did not improve, the country would continue to suffer from disease.

He then toured India by rail, again rallying support for the fight in South Africa. At the same time, he was awakened to the suffering of India's poor. He traveled in third-class trains so that he could experience the way ordinary Indians lived and traveled. He found the trains crowded, dirty, and overpriced. The passengers were treated like animals. Even third-class trains in South Africa were safer and more comfortable.

Gopal Krishna Gokhale, a leader in the Indian National Congress, persuaded Gandhi to settle in Bombay and help with the Congress's legal work. But Gandhi was soon called back to the fight in South Africa. Leaving his family in Bombay, he returned to Durban.

SIMPLICITY AND SATYAGRAHA

Gandhi resumed his law practice in South Africa, but his real work involved the struggle for Indian rights. He cofounded a weekly magazine called *Indian Opinion*, published both in English and Gujarati, Gandhi's native language. His interest in the Hindu religion grew, and he studied the Hindu holy books, with a particular interest in the Bhagavad Gita. He studied the original Sanskrit writings, memorizing them and repeating a few stanzas every morning as he did his ablutions.

The Bhagavad Gita convinced Gandhi that possessions did not matter. He let his life insurance policies lapse. God would take care of his family after he died, he believed. He wrote his brother Laxmidas, who had supported him in earlier years, saying that he would no longer send money to the family. Any savings he had would be used for the benefit of the Indian community. Laxmidas could not understand his brother's attitude. He believed that it was the responsibility of fortunate members of a family to care for the less fortunate members. Unable to agree, the two brothers stopped nearly all communications.

In 1903 Gandhi read a copy of John Ruskin's *Unto This Last,* a book that celebrated the simple life of farming. After sitting up all night reading it, Gandhi decided to buy a one-hundred-acre farm near the city of Phoenix, near Durban. The family joined him there. He moved the presses and equipment for *Indian Opinion* to the farm and also set up a law practice in Johannesburg. His time was divided between the city and the farm, where he grew mango and orange trees.

The Tolstoy Farm, near Johannesburg, South Africa, was the second farm Gandhi established in South Africa.

Gandhi also continued his search for asceticism, or self-denial for spiritual discipline. He practiced fasting and gave up certain foods, such as milk. The result was catastrophic. He developed intestinal wounds that would not heal. He was slowly bleeding to death internally. A doctor persuaded him to drink goat's milk, which saved his life.

Adopting the way of the Brahman, he practiced celibacy. Kasturbai approved of his decision, and their relationship actually improved as a result. The marriage was no longer based on lust and jealousy but instead became a solid friendship. A short time later, Gandhi abandoned Western dress for the simple cotton clothing of his Hindu countrymen.

In August 1906, the *Transvaal Government Gazette* published the draft of an act that would require all Indians except young children to register with and submit fingerprints to the government. The punishment for refusal was imprisonment or expulsion. The Indians of the Transvaal already endured a number of oppressive laws and taxes. The registration act was the final insult. At a mass meeting in Johannesburg's Imperial Theatre on September 11, Gandhi called on his audience to resist.

He called his method of resistance *satyagraha*, which means "insistence on truth." In a broader sense, satyagraha means passive resistance, or nonviolent civil disobedience. The Indians would not fight their adversaries but would simply refuse to cooperate with them. Through nonviolent resistance, Gandhi believed, justice would prevail.

SEVEN-YEAR STRUGGLE

When the registration act was passed on July 31, 1907, Gandhi led the Indians of the Transvaal in resistance. He and many others were arrested, convicted, and sent to jail for two months. A year later, on the afternoon of August 16, 1908, two thousand Indians gathered at the Hamidia Mosque in Johannesburg. They threw their registration certificates into a huge pot filled with wax.

By 1909 the situation in the Transvaal was grim. At one point, as many as 2,500 of the 13,000 Indians in the state had been jailed. Six thousand others had fled the Transvaal. Gandhi had been arrested on several occasions. He had also traveled to England to discuss the South African situation with British leaders. In doing so, he succeeded in making the South African question an international issue.

The conflict came to a head in late 1913. On the morning of November 6, Gandhi and a group of 2,200 Indian men, women, and children began a march to the Tolstoy Farm. This colony near Johannesburg was home to Indians working for the freedom movement. Transvaal border guards let the marchers cross, but Gandhi was arrested. The march continued without him. Meanwhile, Indian miners went on strike (stopped work). To show support for the strikers,

Gandhi in Johannesburg, 1908

other workers went on strike, too. Soon fifty thousand Indian laborers were on strike.

The news of the strike filtered back to India. Charles Hardinge, the British viceroy of India, openly criticized the South African government of General Jan Christian Smuts. Hardinge demanded a commission of inquiry. Smuts refused. Gandhi then announced in late December that he would lead a march from Durban on New Year's Day to invite arrest.

The government was also crippled at this time by a railroad workers' strike and had declared martial law, or military control. All this unrest was too much for Smuts. "You can't put twenty thousand Indians in jail," he said. He opened negotiations with Gandhi.

On June 30, 1914, an agreement was reached. The Indian Relief Bill, which put an end to a number of oppressive measures, was hurried through the South African parliament. Gandhi called the law "the Magna Carta of South African Indians." (The Magna Carta is an English document from the 1200s that became a model for fair systems of justice.) In triumph, he and his wife sailed for England on July 18. Later that year, Rabindranath Tagore, an Indian writer who had won the Nobel Prize for literature in 1913, gave Gandhi the title "Mahatma"—"the Great Soul." He would bear this respectful title forever.

Gandhi and Kasturbai in 1915. Nicknamed Ba, Kasturbai worked alongside her husband during more than sixty years of marriage.

Chapter **FIVE**

TOWARD INDEPENDENCE

GANDHI RETURNED TO INDIA IN JANUARY 1915, already a sort of saint. Everywhere he went, people called out "Mahatma" or "Mahatmaji." He had won freedom for the Indians of South Africa. By this time, all India knew that Gandhi represented their dreams of freedom, too.

The movement for Indian independence had begun in the late nineteenth century. At first, Indian leaders didn't push for complete independence from Britain. They asked only that they be given a hand in running their own country. The Indian National Congress, founded in 1885, took the lead. The congress pressured Britain for more Indian members in governing bodies and for voting rights for upper-class Indians.

But Britain was determined to keep control of its empire and made only small changes.

Gandhi's ideas about Indian independence had evolved in South Africa. Unlike most Indian leaders, Gandhi saw independence as a movement not just for the educated and upper-class Indians. He saw it as a cause for all Indian people, including the poor. Several years earlier, he had written a seventy-six-page pamphlet called *Hind Swaraj*, or *Indian Home Rule*. In it, he explained that Indians could break free of foreign rule only if they united as one people, regardless of religion or social class. "The sword is entirely useless for holding India," he wrote. "We strengthen [the British] hold by quarreling among ourselves."

Eighty percent of India's people lived in small villages. Most were poor and illiterate (unable to read). But Gandhi saw them as crucial in the fight for independence. Once the common people had acquired individual dignity, he argued, they would insist on better living conditions. They would no longer be held in economic bondage.

Gopal Gokhale, leader of the Indian National Congress, had "commanded" Gandhi to spend his first year back in India with his ears open and his mouth shut. Instead, Gandhi made public appearances from the beginning. Wearing only a big turban and a loincloth typical of an Indian peasant, Gandhi appeared on platform after platform, surrounded by Indian politicians in black coats and striped trousers. He urged them to shed these European garments and to adopt native costume. Only in this way, he advised, could politicians reach the hearts of the people.

These same politicians sent petitions to English government officials. This was no way to win independence, Gandhi argued. "No paper contributions will ever give us self-government," he said during a speech in February 1916. "No amount of speeches will make us fit for self-government. It is only our conduct that will fit us for it."

Determined to set the stage for a new Indian society, Gandhi established the Satyagraha ashram near the city of Ahmedabad. The ashram, or religious retreat, was a cluster of whitewashed huts set in a grove of trees. Its members, at first about thirty people, tended fruit trees, spun cotton, wove cloth, prayed, studied, planted and harvested grain, and taught in the neighboring villages. Gandhi lived at the ashram, in a room about the size of a prison cell, for the next sixteen years (when he was not in jail). He often sat among the trees and prayed, reminding people that their nation had known many conquerors and had conquered them all.

THE FIGHT COMES HOME

In December 1916, at the annual convention of the Indian National Congress in the city of Lucknow, Gandhi was approached by a peasant who looked much like all other peasants in India. He was poor and thin. The man introduced himself as Rajkumar Shukla and asked Gandhi to visit his district, Champaran, near the country of Nepal. Farmers there were having trouble with their British landlords, the man explained.

Gandhi truthfully pleaded that he had many other engagements. But Shukla followed him everywhere, even back to the ashram, repeating his plea. Finally, Gandhi gave in and told Shukla to fix a date several months in advance for a meeting in Calcutta. When Gandhi arrived, he found Shukla waiting for him. The two men set out for Champaran.

When they reached the district, Gandhi began to gather information. He visited the British Landlords Association, but the secretary there would give him no facts. He could give no information to an outsider, he said. Gandhi next called on the British commissioner, who bullied him and advised him to leave the district. Gandhi remained and continued his investigation.

He learned that more than one million peasants in the area farmed land they rented from British owners. By a nineteenth-century arrangement, the farmers could grow any crops they wanted. But they had to plant 15 percent of their fields with indigo, used to make dye. The indigo harvest then had to be paid to the landlord as rent for the entire farm. If a farmer stopped growing indigo, the rent could be raised.

This arrangement continued until the early years of the twentieth century. Then, German dye manufacturers developed synthetic indigo, and the market for natural indigo collapsed. Landlords forbade their peasants to grow indigo. But at the same time, they raised rents. The peasants objected. The landlords bullied and beat them, looted their houses, and seized their livestock. Under pressure, thousands of peasants agreed to rent increases. The trouble had begun several years earlier, and there was still no end to it, Gandhi learned.

One day, he was riding an elephant on a country road, when a policeman approached and escorted him back to town. There, Gandhi was served with an official notice to get out of Champaran. He signed the order but wrote on the back that he would disobey.

He was summoned to court. On the day of the hearing, the courthouse square was jammed with villagers. Gandhi had come to help them, and now he was in trouble. Inside the courtroom, Gandhi pleaded guilty to disregarding the order to leave Champaran. He had obeyed the higher order of his conscience, he explained.

Although the case was eventually dropped, the Champaran affair took up a year of Gandhi's time. In the end, the landlords agreed not to increase rents and to refund some of the money they had already collected. Civil disobedience had won for the first time in India. "What I did," Gandhi said, "was a very ordinary thing: I declared that the British could not order me around in my own country." The Champaran incident set the stage for a typical Gandhi pattern. It began as an effort to help the poor. It ended in victory.

Gandhi returned to the ashram but was soon caught

up in another struggle in the people's interest. The mill hands of Ahmedabad had gone on strike after the mill owners refused to negotiate a workplace dispute. Gandhi supported the strikers.

For the first two weeks of the strike, the mill hands exhibited great courage and self-restraint. But then their resolve to practice satyagraha began to weaken. Threats were heard against strikers who returned to work. Gandhi was concerned that the strike would fail.

One morning at a meeting with the mill hands, a light suddenly flashed before Gandhi's eyes. He experienced what the Japanese call *satori* (enlightenment). These words came to his lips: "Unless the strikers rally and continue the strike until a settlement is reached, or till they leave the mills altogether, I will not touch any food."

The mill hands were thunderstruck. They offered to fast with Gandhi, but he refused. The mill owners, worried that Gandhi would become a martyr to the workers' cause, began a furious round of negotiations. An agreement was reached in three days. Gandhi had discovered the fast as a political weapon.

BROKEN PROMISES

As World War I raged in Europe, the movement for Indian self-rule was building. On August 20, 1917, the British secretary of state for India, Sir Edwin S. Montagu, promised a series of reforms. The new measures would increase the number of Indian representatives in every branch of government and would grant self-government to some Indian institutions.

But when the war ended, Britain did not honor its promise. Instead of self-government, India got the Rowlatt Acts—passed on March 18, 1919. These acts continued restrictions on civil liberties that had been passed at the beginning of the war. Those suspected of sedition—stirring up rebellion—could be jailed without trial. Indian leaders, Gandhi included, protested, but in vain. The British government was not listening.

Gandhi had long supported the British Empire. When World War I began, he championed the British ideals of freedom. He raised an ambulance corps of Indian soldiers to help the British armed forces. To those who criticized Gandhi for recruiting soldiers while supporting nonviolence, he replied, "Partnership in the Empire is our definite goal. If the Empire perishes, with it perish our cherished aspirations."

With passage of the Rowlatt Acts, however, Gandhi's loyalty toward Britain began to fall away. He met with dozens of Indian leaders and proposed a satyagraha campaign and a *hartal,* or general economic strike. Throughout India, business came to a standstill. Gandhi fasted for three days. He was proud of the strikers—until he discovered that some of them had become violent. Many British people living in India had been killed.

In retaliation, on April 13, 1919, British-led troops

Gandhi addresses a crowd at an outdoor meeting in Calcutta, India.

killed more than 350 unarmed Indians in the district of Amritsar and wounded 1,100 others. Aghast at the massacre, British leaders tried to make amends. They allowed the Indian National Congress to hold its yearly meeting in December of that year at the site of the killings. King George V also announced the Montagu-Chelmsford reforms, by which Indians would gain control of some provincial governments. The king promised a new era. Many members of the Indian National Congress believed him, adopting a resolution in favor of the Montagu-Chelmsford reforms.

But some Indian leaders were not so trusting. One was Mohammed Ali Jinnah, leader of the Muslim Nationalists. This group wanted to create a separate and self-governing state for India's Muslims. Jinnah opposed the Montagu-Chelmsford reforms, and many Hindus joined him. Postwar disappointment with British promises was starting to run high. It increased after Lord Chelmsford, viceroy of India, acquitted the general who had led the Amritsar Massacre.

The British continued to promise freedom and reforms, but these were not forthcoming. Finally, even Gandhi turned against the British Empire. His emphasis shifted to complete freedom for India.

BOYCOTT

Gandhi was very skilled at sensing the mood of the times. He knew that when people were unhappy they would act. If he did not shape their actions, people might turn violent. He proposed a campaign of noncooperation and a boycott of all things British—goods, courts, schools, and jobs. At a convention in December 1920, Gandhi promised that if the noncooperation campaign remained nonviolent, self-government would arrive in a year.

Many Indian leaders joined the campaign. Jawaharlal Nehru and other prominent lawyers quit practicing in the British courts. University students left their classes, and teachers went into the villages to preach noncooperation, including nonpayment of taxes.

Gandhi then took his campaign nationwide, sometimes accompanied by Muslim leaders. For seven months, he toured India by train, making speeches at every stop. He told people that they should not wear foreign clothing. To support India's cloth factories, he began spinning cotton thread for an hour each day.

The drive for noncooperation continued for a year. Thousands of people were imprisoned for political offenses. But self-government did not arrive as Gandhi had promised. Many leaders, disappointed with Gandhi, called for an open rebellion against Britain. Young people especially demanded action. But Gandhi detested violence, and he continued to argue for peaceful resistance. The Indian National Congress, realizing that Gandhi's approval was critical to the independence movement, upheld the campaign of civil disobedience and agreed not to act without his consent.

In February 1922, Gandhi was leading a protest in Bardoli near Bombay. Word came that a mob had murdered twenty-two police officers in a town eight hundred miles away. Fearful of spreading unrest, Gandhi canceled the campaign in Bardoli and prohibited defiance of the government anywhere in India.

Gandhi was arrested soon after. Lord Reading, then viceroy, regretted the arrest but was under pressure from the British government to make the arrest. Gandhi was charged with three counts of sedition. He offered no defense.

Before sentencing, the judge bowed to Gandhi and

addressed him. "It would be impossible to ignore the fact that in the eyes of millions of your countrymen, you are a great patriot and a great leader," he said. "Even those who differ from you in politics, look upon you as a man of high ideals and of noble and even saintly life." The judge then pronounced the sentence—six years in prison.

Most of the spectators in the courtroom fell at Gandhi's feet and wept. As he was led away, Gandhi smiled. This was not the last time that he would be jailed by the British Raj. But it was the last time the Raj would have the courage to try him in court.

Gandhi recuperates after surgery to remove his appendix in 1924.

Chapter **SIX**

CONTINUED CAMPAIGNS

GANDHI **DID NOT SERVE HIS FULL SIX-YEAR**
sentence for sedition. At Yeravda Central Jail, he developed appendicitis and had to undergo surgery. His
recovery was slow. The British feared that Gandhi
would die while in jail. Fearing public anger they
freed him early, after only twenty-two months in
prison, in February 1924.

The nonviolent protest movement weakened during
Gandhi's stay in prison. Many lawyers who had
stopped practicing in British courts returned to work.
Many students who had left the university resumed
their studies. Gandhi disapproved of their actions.
He remained unchanged in opposing the British
government.

For the next few years, he edited *Young India,* an English-language magazine, and *Navajivan,* a magazine written in Gujarati. Through these publications he argued against the British government, urging non-cooperation and nonviolence. He also addressed the divide between Hindu and Muslim Indians. If the two groups united, Gandhi believed, they could bring about Indian independence.

In the 750,000 villages of India, Muslims and Hindus generally lived peacefully side by side. In the armed forces, they soldiered together. But religious differences often washed out cultural similarities. Competition for limited jobs increased the tension.

In September 1924, Gandhi planned an action that he hoped would draw Hindus and Muslims together. He undertook a three-week fast. During that time, he only drank water. The fast took place in the house of a Muslim friend, and it was meant as a plea for Hindu-Muslim unity.

During the fast, Gandhi wrote some words that showed how his beliefs had shifted over time. Earlier, he had directed his arguments to the English. He had since given up on them, and he directed his message to Indians. When India becomes whole, it will be free.

CONGRESSIONAL TUG OF WAR

The years between 1925 and 1929 were a time of introspection for Gandhi—and little political activity. He lived in the ashram. By then the ashram had become a holy destination for Hindu pilgrims (worshipers) and tourists. Instead of making speeches, Gandhi spun cotton thread. When he did travel, it was usually to encourage the spinning industry. He believed the

Gandhi spins cotton at the Satyagraha ashram in 1925. To boost India's economy, Gandhi urged Indians to make their own cloth and to boycott clothing made by the British.

spinning industry was the key to India's economic freedom from Britain.

But while Gandhi looked inward, much of India was restless. In the former province Bengal, Subhas Chandra Bose, a radical congressman, told his followers, "Give me blood and I promise you freedom." Thousands of supporters flocked to him, particularly young people. Radicals also rallied around congressional leader Jawaharlal Nehru, who preached "Independence Now." Bloody revolution threatened.

At the congressional convention in Calcutta in December 1928, Bose and Nehru dominated the proceedings. They supported a declaration of independence and were not frightened by the idea of a bloody war. Gandhi managed to secure a one-year waiting period as a warning to the British, but only by agreeing to the radical independence proposal.

Gandhi was encouraged by the victory of Britain's Labour Party in the elections of 1929 and to see Ramsay MacDonald named as Britain's new prime minister. MacDonald was a firm supporter of Indian freedom. He called for a roundtable conference of British and Indian delegates to discuss a self-governing Indian state.

Almost immediately, British government leaders attacked MacDonald's policy. On December 23, 1929, Lord Irwin, viceroy of India, had to backtrack in an interview with hopeful Indian leaders. Nothing had been decided.

Ramsay MacDonald supported Gandhi and the struggle for India's independence.

A MARCH TO THE SEA

The Indian National Congress had had enough. That month, at the congressional convention in Lahore, the flag of Indian independence was unfurled. Congress called for secession (separation) from the British Empire and a new campaign of civil disobedience.

Gandhi took charge of the campaign. But first, he approached Lord Irwin with a list of grievances. The most serious of these was the salt tax. All salt in India

Marchers following Gandhi's lead gather salt directly from the Arabian Sea. This was an act against the British Salt Laws.

was supplied by the government. People were required to pay a yearly salt tax that equaled three days' income for a typical peasant. If the government would not negotiate, Gandhi warned, he would begin a march on March 11, 1930, from Ahmedabad to the Arabian Sea (on India's west coast) to challenge the tax. Lord Irwin did not reply.

March 11 arrived. For the next 24 days, Gandhi and

his followers marched. On April 5, they reached the sea at Dandi. By this time, Gandhi's group was several thousand strong. He walked into the ocean and picked up a handful of sea salt, breaking the law against possession of salt not purchased from the government.

All along India's long seacoast, villagers followed Gandhi's lead and picked up sea salt. The police made mass arrests. Congressional leaders, including Jawaharlal Nehru, were sentenced to prison for breaking the salt law. Soon, sixty thousand Indians were in jail on political charges.

Gandhi was arrested on May 4. Hundreds of others were arrested in a raid on the Dharasana Salt Works, a processing plant 150 miles north of Bombay. Gandhi's son Manilal led the action there. Police beat and kicked the marchers, who had been instructed against violence. The 2,500 marchers were beaten about the head with steel staffs. They bled and fell. But they did not raise a hand against their attackers. "When the Indians allowed themselves to be beaten with batons and rifle butts and did not cringe, they showed that England was powerless, and India invincible," wrote Gandhi biographer Louis Fischer.

TO ENGLAND

Gandhi was in jail when a roundtable conference was finally held in London to discuss problems in India. Because most of India's congressmen were also in jail, the conference failed completely. As a result, Indian

INDIA'S CASTE SYSTEM

When Mohandas Gandhi called for equal treatment of India's untouchables, or harijans (children of God) as he called them, he was challenging a strict and centuries-old Hindu tradition: the caste system. According to Hindu belief, a person's caste is set by birth and cannot be changed. Caste determines a person's rights and status in Indian society, with the Brahmans holding the top spot.

The Brahmans also claimed the highest spiritual purity. To remain pure, Hindus must not eat any food or do work that would pollute, or defile, them. First and foremost, orthodox (strict) Hindus must never eat meat, particularly beef. Any occupation that involves killing animals or handling their skins—leatherwork or shoemaking, for instance—is thought to be polluting. Other polluting work is cleaning human waste, handling dead bodies, even washing clothes. Traditionally, such work is left to the untouchables.

The untouchables are India's outcastes. They do not belong to any caste and stand below every other group in the social hierarchy. They make up about 15 percent of India's population. For centuries, the untouchables were forced to live on the outskirts of towns, forbidden to draw water from communal wells, and forbidden to enter temples.

Gandhi's campaign on behalf of the harijans changed all this— but ancient traditions did not disappear overnight. Although India's 1950 constitution forbids discrimination against harijans and grants them equal rights, prejudice and segregation remain, even into the twenty-first century.

However, as India becomes more urban and industrialized, members of all Hindu castes interact with one another in neighborhoods and workplaces. Ancient restrictions and caste divisions have begun to fall away.

leaders were freed, and Gandhi met with Lord Irwin.
At the meeting, Gandhi wanted equal status for India
within the British Commonwealth (an association of
former British colonies, including Australia and Canada,
that had recently been granted self-government).

He traveled to England in 1931, the sole delegate representing the Indian congress to the second roundtable. He dressed in what had become his usual
costume—a loincloth, shawl, sandals, and a dangling
watch. He even wore the costume when visiting Buckingham Palace in London, where he was received by
King George V for tea.

Gandhi was back in India when a new government
came to power in London that fall. Ramsay
MacDonald was again prime minister, but many other
offices had changed. Lord Willingdon replaced Lord
Irwin as viceroy. Willingdon promptly declared a
state-of-emergency in India, throwing most congressional leaders into jail for obstructing the British
government.

Once again, Gandhi landed in Yeravda Central Jail,
this time with Jawaharlal Nehru and other leaders of
the independence movement. It was there that Gandhi
conceived of a new campaign for freedom. The cause
would be India's untouchables. Gandhi called them
harijans, children of God.

Gandhi is surrounded by smiling people in London, 1931.
Gandhi was always friendly and approachable wherever he went.

Chapter SEVEN

CHILDREN OF GOD

INDIA'S UNTOUCHABLES NUMBERED ABOUT 60 MILLION in the 1930s. For centuries, they had been the outcastes of Indian society. They were not allowed in Hindu temples. They lived in the worst urban slums and on the filthy outskirts of villages. They performed menial occupations—sweeping streets, scrubbing floors, cleaning toilets. In some areas, even the shadow of an untouchable was regarded as unclean.

Some untouchables escaped their fates by converting to Christianity or Islam. Others were able to gain educations and good jobs, despite the prejudices leveled against them by upper-class Indians. A group of educated untouchables, led by Dr. Bhimrao Ramji Ambedkar, began a movement to abolish India's caste system altogether. But most untouchables held to the Hindu belief that they were being punished for wickedness in previous lives. They accepted their fates and hoped that they would be elevated to higher positions after death.

Early in life, Gandhi accepted the caste system as a traditional part of Hindu society. But over the years, he had come to sympathize more and more with the outcastes. He saw no difference between Britain's exploitation of India and India's exploitation of its untouchables. By the time of his jailing in 1932, Gandhi was ready to rebel against the untouchables' "separation from the Hindu fold."

India was already suffering from religious infighting. Muslim leaders were lobbying Britain for their own representatives within a new Indian government. A British measure, proposed in August 1932, would have created separate representation for the untouchables

Gandhi reached out to help the untouchables and worked to end their inhumane treatment.

too—they would be separated from other Hindus as a distinct electorate, or voting group.

But Gandhi sought a united India, without separate electorates. He announced that if the British measure passed, he would begin a fast—unto death if need be—at noon on September 20, 1932. The fast was not directed against the British government, Gandhi said. It was aimed at the Hindu community, because Hindus refused to give untouchables humane treatment.

At 11:30 A.M. on September 20, Gandhi took his last sustenance, a glass of hot water with honey and lemon juice. That evening, his friend Rabindranath Tagore addressed a school near Calcutta. "A shadow is darkening over India," he said. "Mahatmaji, who through his life of sacrifice has made India his own, has commenced his vow of supreme self-sacrifice.... No civilized society can thrive upon victims whose humanity has been permanently mutilated. Against that deep-seated moral weakness in our society Mahatmaji has pronounced his ultimatum."

Immediately, Hindu leaders in Bombay met with untouchable leaders, led by Bhimrao Ambedkar. He at first called Gandhi's fast "a political stunt" but then began to listen. The leaders hammered out a plan that would give the untouchables much more representation in government than had been proposed by the British. More important, the untouchables would not be separated from other Hindus as a voting group.

After Ambedkar tentatively approved the plan, the

Rabindranath Tagore, an Indian writer who gave Gandhi the title "Mahatma," or "the Great Soul," was a longtime supporter of Gandhi and his work.

Hindu leaders took the night train to the Yeravda jail to present the matter to Gandhi. He had grown weak from fasting—so weak that he had to be carried to the toilet on a stretcher. Doctors examined Gandhi's heart and said he might die at any moment. But he asked questions of the negotiators and accepted the plan. It was sent on to London that weekend for approval by the British government.

A CHANGE OF HEART

Meanwhile, word of the fast raced across India. With the news that Gandhi was nearing death, a sense of urgency seized the cities. The Kalighat Temple of Calcutta announced that it was opening its doors to untouchables for the first time in thousands of years. So did the Ram Mandir Temple of Benares, regarded as the center of traditional Hinduism. All across India, temples threw open their doors. Prominent Brahmans and other Hindus dined publicly with untouchables. At universities, classes and dining rooms were opened to them. In Bombay, a women's organization conducted a poll in front of seven temples. Ballot boxes were set up and votes counted. The vote was twenty-seven thousand for allowing untouchables into the temples and only five hundred against.

Practically overnight, Gandhi's fast and the pact signed at Yeravda jail broke a chain of injustice that stretched back thousands of years. The Monday after the agreement arrived in London, the British government announced its acceptance of the plan.

With the harijan campaign completed, Gandhi retreated from political life once again. He concentrated instead on helping India's poor. Based at an ashram in Sevagram, a village in central India, he promoted social programs for improving education and sanitation.

Gandhi lived a spiritual, modest life of prayer, fasting, and meditation. He strove to help others and to leave a better, more peaceful world behind.

Chapter **EIGHT**

THE FINAL
CAMPAIGN

THE **INDIAN INDEPENDENCE MOVEMENT HEATED UP**
once more during World War II. As part of the British
Empire, India automatically entered the conflict when
Great Britain went to war with Germany in September 1939. While Adolf Hitler's forces attacked Britain
and marched through the rest of Europe, Japan was
also expanding its Asian empire and threatening India
from the east.

Gandhi was opposed to aggression and aggressive
governments, and he supported the British fight. But
this time, he would give moral support only. He would
not recruit troops or medical personnel as he had during the Boer War and World War I. Nor would he
fight the Japanese, who stood at the gates of India at

the cities of Imphal and Kohima by the spring of 1942. Instead, Gandhi suggested passive resistance. "Neither food nor shelter is to be given [to the Japanese army]," he said, "nor any dealings to be established with them. They should be made to feel that they are not wanted. The people must evacuate the infested place in order to deny compulsory service to the enemy."

Only a few pacifist (antiviolence) congressmen followed Gandhi's lead. The majority would have gone to war willingly for a price—Indian independence. Jawaharlal Nehru put it plainly. "I would fight Japan, sword in hand," he said, "But I can do so only as a free man."

"Quit India"

The war was, in some ways, a contest between Mohandas Gandhi and Winston Churchill, who became British prime minister in 1940. Churchill was determined that Britain should not lose control of India. In November 1942, he stated, "I did not become the King's first minister to preside at the liquidation of the British Empire."

The struggle between Gandhi and Churchill had been going on for many years. "Gandhism and all it stands for must ultimately be grappled with and finally crushed," Churchill had said many years earlier. During the war years, he made his feelings even plainer. "We intend to hold our own," he said.

Prime Minister Winston Churchill was strongly opposed to Gandhi and independence for India.

Churchill was responsible for the failure of Sir Stafford Cripps, who, in March 1942, had sought Indian participation in the struggle against Hitler. The price would be some degree of independence, Indian leaders told him. Cripps was willing to pay that price, but Churchill was not. American president Franklin Roosevelt tried to step in on behalf of Cripps and the campaign for Indian liberty. But Churchill still had visions of Gandhi striding up the stairs of Buckingham Palace to share power with the king, and he would have none of it. He put an end to the negotiations.

Gandhi began an antigovernment movement in June. He called on the British to "quit India"—to withdraw from the nation entirely. His effort went nowhere. In frustration, Gandhi proposed a new campaign of civil disobedience. Jawaharlal Nehru and Maulana Azad, then president of the Indian National Congress, opposed the idea. But Gandhi insisted. Congress, meeting in Bombay, backed Gandhi's call for civil disobedience on August 7. He spoke on the night of August 8. "Every one of you, from this instant consider himself a free man," he told the congressmen, "and even act as if you were free and no longer under the heel of imperialism."

Before dawn on August 9, Gandhi and all the major leaders of Congress were in prison. Gandhi's call for civil disobedience had not yet been issued. On August 9, anti-British violence erupted. Crowds of Indians set fire to police stations and government buildings. They ripped up rail lines, destroyed telegraph lines, assaulted, and in some cases killed, officials. In some areas, "free Indian governments" were established.

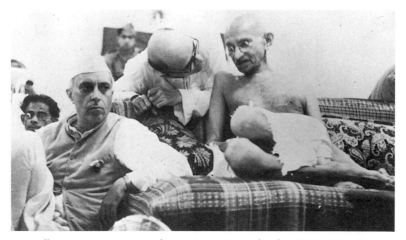

Gandhi, seated at right, *his secretary Mahader Desai,* middle, *and Jawaharlal Nehru,* seated at left. *Not long after this photo was taken, the three men were jailed during the "Quit India" campaign.*

The British blamed the violence on Gandhi. He bombarded officials in India and England with evidence showing that he was not responsible for the destruction and death. He accused the government of distortions and misrepresentations. The idea that he, the leader of the nonviolence movement, was accused of promoting violence angered Gandhi. But he was virtually helpless in prison, and he could not publicly argue against the false information. Nor could he stop the violence.

Finally, Gandhi declared that he would begin a three-week fast. The viceroy accused him of political blackmail. Two days before the scheduled fast, the viceroy offered to release Gandhi and his colleagues. Gandhi refused. He was not fasting to win release from prison, he said, he was fasting "in an appeal to the Highest Tribunal for justice, which I have failed to secure from you."

Gandhi was still in prison when Kasturbai died in February 1944. Six weeks later, Gandhi suffered an attack of malaria, which made him delirious. Supporters began demanding his release. The government, expecting more violence, placed a heavy guard around the prison. On May 6, 1944, Gandhi and his associates were finally released.

Gandhi returned to politics. He first sought a meeting with Archibald Wavell, the new viceroy. But Gandhi's old adversary, Winston Churchill, was still prime minister. The effort to arrange the meeting failed. Wavell rejected the request. Gandhi then wrote to Mohammed Ali Jinnah, president of the Muslim League, asking that Hindus and Muslims present a united front to the British. Gandhi appealed to Jinnah as a fellow Indian and addressed him by the title Qaid-e-Azam—"Great Leader." But Jinnah responded coldly, and after three weeks of correspondence, Gandhi gave up. Jinnah was set on the division of India into two nations, one Hindu and one Muslim. Gandhi stood fast for one India.

In May 1945, Germany surrendered to the Allies, and the European part of the war was over. After many years of war, the British people wanted change, and the Labour Party won decisively in national elections. Clement Attlee replaced Winston Churchill as prime minister.

By this time, Britain viewed India as more of a problem than an asset to its empire. So one of the Labour government's first moves was to announce that it would grant self-government to India.

THE FIGHT WITHIN

But independence would not be established without another fight. Mohammed Ali Jinnah still demanded the partition (division) of India into two nations, Hindu and Muslim. The Muslim nation would be called Pakistan. "We could settle the Indian question in ten minutes," Jinnah said, "if Mr. Gandhi would say I agree that there should be Pakistan." Jinnah proposed that one-fourth of India—the provinces of Sind, Baluchistan, the Punjab, the Northwest Frontier, Bengal, and Assam—would form Pakistan.

Gandhi would not agree. For forty years, he had worked for a united India. Anything else was unacceptable to him. He regarded Jinnah's proposal as blasphemy.

So the two adversaries were pitted against each other. Jinnah appealed to the fears of middle-class Muslims. He said that a united India would be ruled by Hindus. They would get the best government jobs and would repress fellow Muslim citizens. Gandhi argued for a united and secular India, dominated by neither religious group.

A British commission, arriving in India on March 23,

Muslim leader Mohammed Ali Jinnah was set on the division of India into separate Muslim and Hindu nations.

1946, examined the Hindu-Muslim dispute. The commission found evidence that almost all Indians wanted a united state. But the British also recognized the fears of the Muslim minority.

The commission examined the case for a separate Muslim state, but found problems with the idea. Jinnah wanted an independent Pakistan so that Muslims

PAKISTAN AND BANGLADESH

When British leaders granted Indian independence in 1947, they also acknowledged the Muslim call for independence, creating the state of Pakistan. The new state was made up of two separate pieces of territory—one from northwestern India and one from northeastern India. Mohammed Ali Jinnah, longtime leader of the Muslim League, became Pakistan's first head of government.

Although the Muslims had realized their goal of a separate nation, free from Hindu control, problems surfaced. East and West Pakistan were separated by one thousand miles, and the people of the two sections had little in common except the Islamic religion. Cultural and language differences drove a wedge between the two halves. In addition, many East Pakistanis felt that West Pakistan had an unfair share of control over the nation's government, business affairs, and military forces.

Tensions brewed for years and, in 1971, finally erupted into civil war. In December 1971, after months of fighting and more than one million deaths, East Pakistan broke free from West Pakistan, creating the independent nation of Bangladesh.

would not be ruled by Hindus. But Assam province, which Jinnah demanded for Pakistan, had only 3.4 million Muslims and 6.7 million non-Muslims. In the Punjab, the Muslims numbered 16 million, non-Muslims 12 million. Of Bengal's 60 million people, 52 percent were Muslims, 48 percent were non-Muslims. Jinnah's plan would leave 20 million Muslims under Hindu rule and 47 million Hindus and Sikhs under Muslim rule. What's more, the commission noted, the two halves of the proposed state of Pakistan would be separated from one another by one thousand miles of Indian territory. Communications between the two sections, in war and peace, would have to rely on the goodwill of the Hindu state.

The commission returned to London and advised the British government against dividing India. Instead, it recommended creating a weak central Indian government and three strong regional governments. The first region, Section A, would include the mostly Hindu provinces of central India. Section B would contain the heavily Muslim provinces of western India. Section C would include the provinces of Bengal (mostly Muslim) and Assam (mostly Hindu) in the northeast of India. The regional governments would have wide areas of authority. The central government would be responsible for national defense, foreign affairs, and communications.

The Muslim League argued long and hard against the British plan, but finally accepted it. Gandhi and the Indian National Congress debated the proposal endlessly. They were suspicious of the British and in the end refused to accept the proposal. With that, Jinnah also withdrew the Muslim League's acceptance of the plan and returned to the demand for a separate Pakistan.

"DO OR DIE"

Instead of ushering in a new independent government, India erupted into violence. On August 16, 1946, the Muslims of Calcutta rose in an attack on Hindus. In four days, five thousand people were killed and fifteen thousand wounded. In response, Hindus murdered Muslims in the Punjab, Bombay, Bihar, and Bengal regions. Racial violence led to class violence. In Calcutta, untouchables were beaten when they tried to draw water from community wells.

In October, in the remote Noakhali region of Bengal, Muslims were killing Hindu men and raping Hindu women. In response, in the heavily Hindu province of Bihar, Hindus proclaimed October 25 to be Noakhali Day and paraded through the streets shouting "Blood for Blood." In the following week, according to the *London Times*, 4,580 people were killed by rioters. Gandhi later put the total at more than ten thousand, most of them Muslims.

After a time, the violence let up, and Gandhi went to Noakhali to offer support for the Hindus there. "I am not going to leave Bengal," he told a prayer meeting,

Race riots broke out in August 1946 in Calcutta, leaving many people dead and the city in ruins.

"until the last embers of the trouble are stamped out. I may stay here for a year or more."

From November 1946 to March 1947, Gandhi lived in Noakhali, talking and praying with the people there. He rose at four in the morning and walked from village to village, sometimes barefoot. Often, hostile Muslims threw filth in his path. But he did not blame them, he said, for they had been misled by their politicians. "My present mission is the most difficult and complicated one of my life," he said. "Hindus and Muslims should learn to live together in peace and amity. Otherwise I should die in the attempt."

During the period of violence surrounding the partition of India, Gandhi visited many communities to spread his message of peace and unity.

Chapter NINE

INDEPENDENCE AT LAST

ON AUGUST 15, 1947, BRITAIN FINALLY GRANTED
independence to India. But religious differences had
won out: India was to be divided into separate Hindu
and Muslim states—India and Pakistan. But as earlier
studies had shown, there was no way to divide the nation cleanly along religious lines. The division created
terror and chaos for those Hindus who found themselves suddenly living in the Muslim nation and vice
versa. Violence again raged throughout India.

Gandhi, concerned about rioting in Calcutta, decided
to begin a fast. Unless sanity returned to the city,
Gandhi said, he would die. The fast began on the
evening of September 1. Within a few hours, word had
spread through the city. Groups of people began calling

at the house where Gandhi was staying. They would do anything to save Gandhi's life, they proclaimed. That was the wrong goal, he answered. Saving his life was not important. A change of heart was important. So both Muslim and Hindu leaders pledged that they would work together for peace. That was not enough either, said Gandhi. They must put the pledges in writing.

The city rallied around Gandhi. Five hundred police officers began a one-day fast in sympathy with him. Groups of merchants, longshoremen, city workers, and other citizens signed pledges to keep the peace. On September 4, 1947, the police reported that Calcutta was absolutely quiet—not one sign of violence in twenty-four hours. From that day on, throughout the bloody months that followed elsewhere, Calcutta and other cities in Bengal remained peaceful. Muslims and Hindus kept their pledges.

On September 7, Gandhi left Calcutta to help put down religious massacres in the Punjab and other provinces. Stopping in Delhi, he learned of religious riots there, too. So he left his train and settled in the untouchable quarter of the city, despite warnings that he would not be safe there. Later, he moved to the grand residence of G. D. Birla, one of India's wealthiest industrialists and a longtime Gandhi friend and supporter.

Delhi was like a city of the dead. No vegetables, milk, or fresh fruits were coming into the city. Hindu refugees from Muslim areas of the Punjab were streaming in. Muslim refugees were flooding in on their way to Pakistan. Gandhi spent the next few months moving from one dangerous area to another. He visited Hindu and Muslim refugee camps without guards to protect him. Everywhere, he brought his message of love, and where he went, peace followed.

But sporadic violence continued everywhere except in Bengal. Hindus were being murdered in Pakistan, and Muslims were not safe in India, especially Delhi. It came to Gandhi that it was again time to fast to stir the consciences of the people. He knew he might die. But he welcomed death if it meant he brought peace to India's people.

"I Have Thrown Myself on God"

On January 13, 1948, Gandhi began his fast at the Birla home. On the first day, he walked to a prayer meeting. "I expect a thorough cleansing of hearts," he told his followers. On the second day, doctors advised him not to walk to prayers, so he dictated a message to be read there. But when the time arrived, Gandhi could not resist attending the prayer meeting.

He continued to ignore his doctors. He refused to drink water, and his kidneys began to function poorly. He lost weight and strength. On the fourth day of the fast, doctors warned Gandhi that he faced serious injury to his organs. He did not listen to them and spoke to the prayer meeting by microphone.

On January 17, Gandhi sent an agent to Delhi to see

if it was safe for Muslims to return there. Ever since the fast had begun, Dr. Rajendra Prasad, the new president of India's congress, had been meeting with various groups to bring an end to the violence. Gandhi told him that mere pledges were not enough—not even written pledges.

On January 18, one hundred religious and political leaders came to Gandhi. They guaranteed that Muslims would be safe in India and that they could safely worship at their mosques. Gandhi sat on his cot and thought. He was not quite sure he could trust the men. But one by one they pleaded with him, and he finally agreed to break his fast. He drank a glass of orange juice.

The fast had severely weakened Gandhi. On the first and second days afterward, he had to be carried to prayers in a chair. While he addressed the meeting, a blast was heard. Someone had thrown a bomb. "Don't worry about it," Gandhi said. "Listen to me."

Later, the crowd learned that the bomb had been thrown from a garden wall by a young man. He had been wrestled to the ground by an old woman, who had held him until the police arrived. He was Madan Lal, a Hindu refugee from the Punjab. He talked about the atrocities that he had seen against Hindus by Muslims there. He blamed Gandhi for the troubles.

The next day at the prayer grounds, Gandhi made light of the bombing incident. "No one should look down on the misguided youth who threw the bomb," he

India in the Late 1800s

Kohima
Imphal
ASSAM
NOAKHALI
Calcutta
BENGAL
Bay of Bengal
BIHAR
HIMALAYAS
Delhi
Lucknow
INDIA
Sabarmati R.
Ahmedabad
Porbandar
Bombay
Pune
Indus R.
NORTH-
WEST
FRONTIER
Lahore
AMRITSAR
(PUNJAB)
SIND
Rajkot
GUJARAT
Karachi
BALUCHISTAN
Arabian Sea
N

INDIA
WEST
PAKISTAN
EAST
PAKISTAN
(BANGLADESH)
India and
Pakistan
After 1947

said. "He probably looks upon me as an enemy of Hinduism. You should pity [him] and try to convert him."

But he did not know that other members of a conspiracy to silence him were near. One of them, Nathuram Vinayak Godse, was the editor of a weekly Hindu newspaper in Poona. After the failure of Madan Lal's bomb, Godse began hanging around the Birla house. He carried a Beretta pistol in his pocket. He was angry about the creation of Pakistan and about Gandhi's moral authority over the people.

Gandhi was distressed that two of his associates were quarreling—Jawaharlal Nehru, prime minister of India, and Deputy Prime Minister Sardar Patel. On January 30, Gandhi wrote a note to Nehru saying that the two must not argue. At four in the afternoon, Patel came to see Gandhi and was told the same thing.

While Patel visited, Gandhi ate his supper. Five o'clock came, and he hurried to the prayer ground, leaning on the shoulders of two female followers. "I am late by ten minutes," he said. "I hate being late. I should have been here on the stroke of five."

He moved forward to the platform where he sat during prayers. Most of the people there rose at his coming. He lifted his arms and put his hands together in the traditional Hindu blessing. He looked around. He was pleased to see that the police officer who had been assigned to guard him was not there. He wanted no guardians.

But Godse was there. He stood up and approached

the Mahatma, his hand on the pistol in his pocket. He bowed to Gandhi in reverence and stepped closer. A woman tried to brush Godse away, so Gandhi could start the service. Godse pushed her away, planted himself two feet in front of Gandhi, and fired three shots.

The smile on Gandhi's face faded. He dropped his arms to his sides and died.

EPILOGUE

Mohandas Gandhi died feeling that he had failed in his mission to create a free and united India. In the case of India, he had failed. But other inspiring leaders came along to pick up the torch—Martin Luther King Jr. in the United States and Nelson Mandela in

Thousands of people lined the streets of Rajkot during Gandhi's funeral on January 31, 1948.

South Africa. Both men used Gandhi's techniques of civil disobedience and nonviolent, passive resistance to protest racial segregation and injustice. King led black Americans in the movement for Civil Rights and integration in the United States. Mandela did the same for blacks in South Africa. Without Gandhi's methods of nonviolent resistance, their successes might have been impossible.

Upon Gandhi's death, the outpouring of grief in India was overwhelming. His influence on the lives of all Indians and on the course of Indian history had been profound.

In the history of freedom, Gandhi's name must be written larger than life. He was, as they say in India, a slice of God.

THE LIFE OF GANDHI

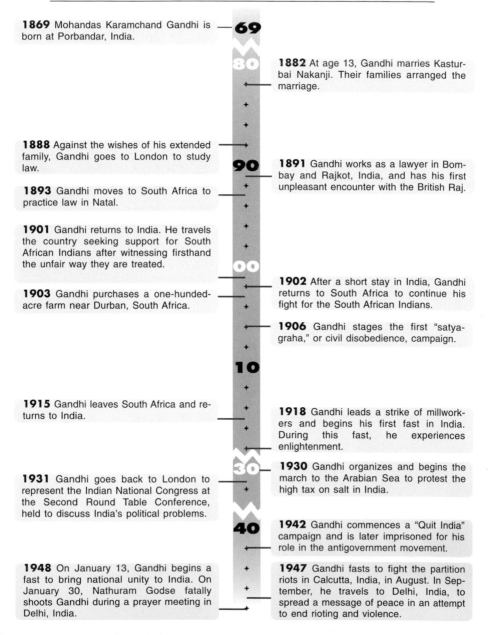

1869 Mohandas Karamchand Gandhi is born at Porbandar, India.

1882 At age 13, Gandhi marries Kasturbai Nakanji. Their families arranged the marriage.

1888 Against the wishes of his extended family, Gandhi goes to London to study law.

1891 Gandhi works as a lawyer in Bombay and Rajkot, India, and has his first unpleasant encounter with the British Raj.

1893 Gandhi moves to South Africa to practice law in Natal.

1901 Gandhi returns to India. He travels the country seeking support for South African Indians after witnessing firsthand the unfair way they are treated.

1902 After a short stay in India, Gandhi returns to South Africa to continue his fight for the South African Indians.

1903 Gandhi purchases a one-hundred-acre farm near Durban, South Africa.

1906 Gandhi stages the first "satyagraha," or civil disobedience, campaign.

1915 Gandhi leaves South Africa and returns to India.

1918 Gandhi leads a strike of millworkers and begins his first fast in India. During this fast, he experiences enlightenment.

1930 Gandhi organizes and begins the march to the Arabian Sea to protest the high tax on salt in India.

1931 Gandhi goes back to London to represent the Indian National Congress at the Second Round Table Conference, held to discuss India's political problems.

1942 Gandhi commences a "Quit India" campaign and is later imprisoned for his role in the antigovernment movement.

1948 On January 13, Gandhi begins a fast to bring national unity to India. On January 30, Nathuram Godse fatally shoots Gandhi during a prayer meeting in Delhi, India.

1947 Gandhi fasts to fight the partition riots in Calcutta, India, in August. In September, he travels to Delhi, India, to spread a message of peace in an attempt to end rioting and violence.

Sources

7   Mohandas K. Gandhi, *The Story of My Experiments with Truth* (Washington, DC: Public Affairs Press, 1948), 97.

12   William L. Shirer, *Gandhi: A Memoir* (New York: Washington Square Press, 1979), 1.

18   Gandhi, 4.

22–24   Ibid., 8, 26–27, 34.

30   Indian folk saying

32   Gandhi, 50.

42–43   Ibid., 101, 121, 122.

45   Ibid., 169.

47   Ibid., 196.

53   Ibid., 150.

53   Louis Fischer, *Gandhi: His Life and Message for the World* (New York: Mentor Books, 1954), 48.

56   Ibid., 52.

57   Ibid., 54.

59   Ibid., 59.

60   Gandhi, 388.

61   Fischer, 57.

65   Ibid., 73

70   Ibid., 93.

73   Ibid., 102.

78–79   Ibid., 115, 117–118.

84   Ibid., 134–136.

86–88   Ibid., 146–147, 149.

92–93   Ibid., 162, 164–165, 183.

98–100   Ibid., 187, 189.

GLOSSARY OF TERMS

ahimsa: the Hindu doctrine of nonviolence toward all living things

ashram: a religious retreat

Bhagavad Gita: a Hindu holy book that sets forth the god Krishna's teachings to the warrior hero Arjuna

Brahman: a Hindu of the highest caste; a priest

civil disobedience: refusal to obey government demands as a means of bringing about social or political change

Gujarati: a language of northwestern India

Hinduism: the dominant religion of India, Hinduism is based on the belief that those who live a good life will be reincarnated into a higher state.

Islam: a religion practiced in India, Pakistan, Bangladesh, and the Middle East, based on the belief in Allah as the sole deity and in Mohammed as his prophet. Adherents of Islam are called Muslims.

Jainism: a religion of India based on the belief that every living thing has an eternal soul and a temporary body

Raj: the former British government of India

Sanskrit: the traditional language of Hinduism

satyagraha: "insistence on truth"; Gandhi's term for bringing about reform through nonviolent resistance

Sikhism: a monotheistic religion founded in India about 1500 and marked by a belief in reincarnation and the rejection of caste.

untouchables: outcastes; Indians born outside the Hindu caste system, traditionally segregated and shunned by the upper castes

SELECTED BIBLIOGRAPHY

Bikhu, Parekh. *Gandhi.* New York: Oxford University Press, 1997.

Bondurant, Joan Valerie. *Conquest of Violence.* Princeton, NJ: Princeton University Press, 1988.

Clement, Catherine. *Gandhi: The Power of Pacifism.* New York: Harry N. Abrams, 1996.

Easwaran, Eknath, and Michael Nagler. *Gandhi, the Man: The Story of His Transformation.* Tomales, CA: Nilgiri Press, 1997.

Fischer, Louis. *Gandhi: His Life and Message for the World.* New York: Mentor Books, 1954.

Gandhi, Mohandas K. *All Men Are Brothers: Autobiographical Reflections.* New York: Continuum Publishing Group, 1980.

_____. *Autobiography: The Story of My Experiments with Truth.* New York: Dover Publications, 1983.

Merton, Thomas. *Gandhi on Non-Violence.* New York: New Directions, 1964.

Settel, Trudy S. *The Book of Gandhi Wisdom.* Sacramento: Citadel Press, 1985.

Severance, John B. *Gandhi, Great Soul.* Boston: Houghton Mifflin, 1997.

Yogish, Chadha. *Gandhi: A Life.* New York: John Wiley and Sons, 1998.

INDEX

OTHER TITLES FROM LERNER AND A&E®:

Arthur Ashe

Bill Gates

Bruce Lee

Carl Sagan

Chief Crazy Horse

Christopher Reeve

Eleanor Roosevelt

George Lucas

Gloria Estefan

Jack London

Jacques Cousteau

Jesse Owens

Jesse Ventura

John Glenn

Legends of Dracula

Legends of Santa Claus

Louisa May Alcott

Madeleine Albright

Maya Angelou

Mother Teresa

Nelson Mandela

Princess Diana

Queen Cleopatra

Queen Latifah

Rosie O'Donnell

Saint Joan of Arc

Wilma Rudolph

Women in Space

Women of the Wild West

ABOUT THE AUTHOR

Christopher Martin has written more than one hundred books over the past thirty years. He received a bachelor's degree from the University of Oregon and now lives in Japan with his wife, Hiroko, an English teacher. Martin developed a keen interest in Mohandas Gandhi after spending time in India in the early 1940s.

PHOTO ACKNOWLEDGMENTS

Photographs used with permission of: Corbis: (© Bettmann) p. 85, (UPI/Bettmann) pp. 62, 86, (© E.O. Hoppé) p. 78, (© Hulton-Deutsch Collection) pp. 80, 93; © DPA/MKG/The Image Works, pp. 2, 6, 8, 10, 13, 14, 16, 20, 25, 33, 38, 40, 45, 49, 52, 54, 66, 69, 82; Archive Photos: (Popperfoto) pp. 31, 76, (Archive) pp. 28, 71, 72, 89, 94; AP/Wide World Photos, p. 102.

Front cover: © Bettmann/Corbis. Back cover: Archive Photos. Map on page 99 by Laura Westlund.